Ages 8+

 LEARNING

Smart S...
Cursive

MW01554654

Carson Dellosa Education
Greensboro, North Carolina

© & ™ 2021 Lucasfilm Ltd.
All rights reserved.

Published by
Carson Dellosa Education
PO Box 35665
Greensboro, NC 27425 USA

Except as permitted under the United States Copyright Act, no part of this publication may be reproduced, stored, or distributed in any form or by any means (mechanically, electronically, recording, etc.) without the prior written consent of Carson Dellosa Education.

Printed in the USA • All rights reserved.
01-053217784

ISBN 978-1-4838-6145-6

Contents

Name 4
Letters Aa—Jj 6
Letters Kk—Rr 26
Letters Ss—Zz 42
Missing Letter Practice 58
Word and Sentence Practice 60
Completion Certificate 64

Smart Skill: Name

Print your name below.

In cursive writing, all lowercase letters connect to the letter that follows. Some uppercase letters join the next letter, and some do not. Follow this guide:

These uppercase letters join the next letter.	These uppercase letters do not join the next letter.
A, C, E, H, J, K, M, N, R, U, Y, Z	B, D, F, G, I, L, O, P, Q, S, T, V, W, X

Let's Go!

Smart Skill: A/a

Anakin Skywalker is ready for anything.

Anakin

Skywalker

anything

Smart Skill: B/b

Boba Fett is a bounty hunter.

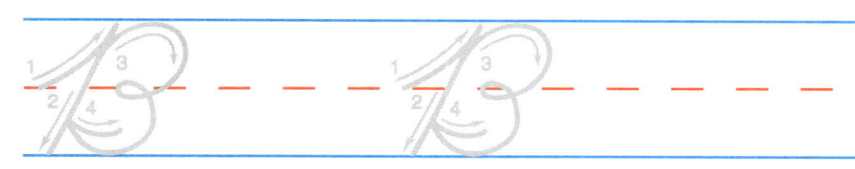

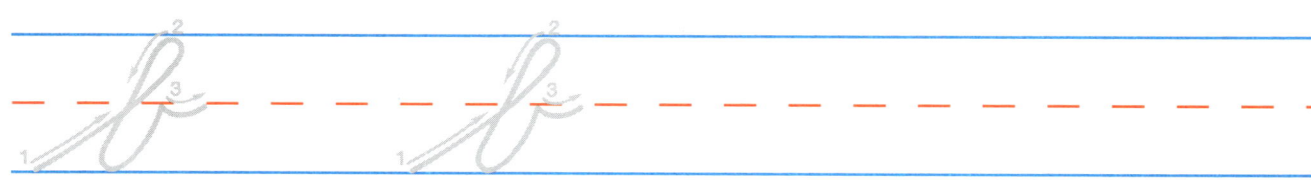

Boba Fett

bounty

Smart Skill: C/c

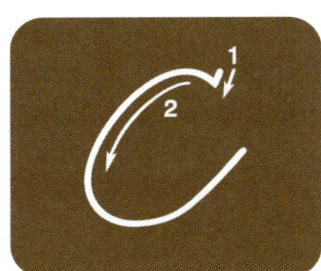

Chewbacca is Han Solo's co-pilot.

Smart Skill: D/d

Droids can be good friends.

Droids can be good friends.

Droids

good

friends

Smart Skill: E/e

Ewoks live on Endor.

Ewoks live on Endor.

Smart Skill: F/f

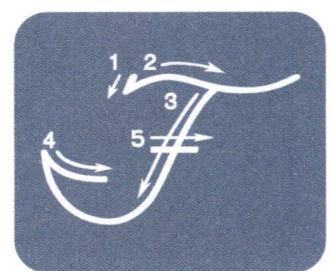

Finn escaped from the First Order.

Finn escaped from the First Order.

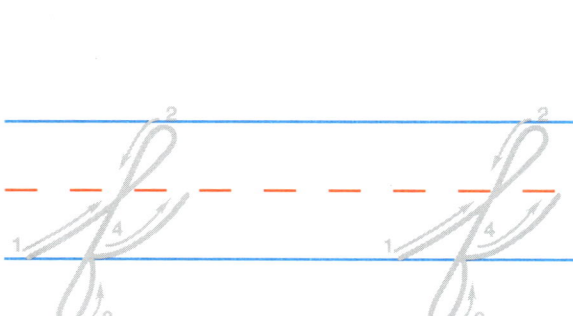

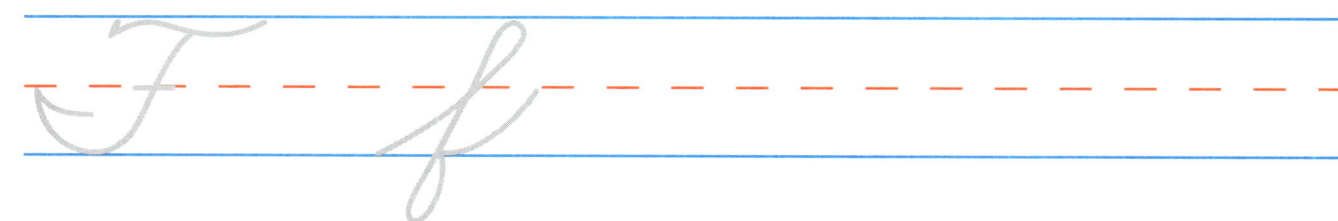

Finn

from

First Order

Smart Skill: G/g

General Leia Organa is a great leader.

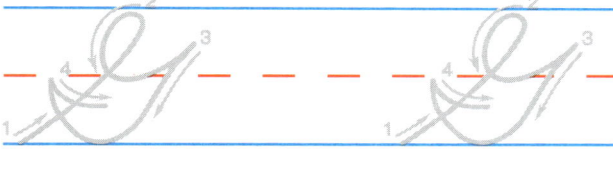

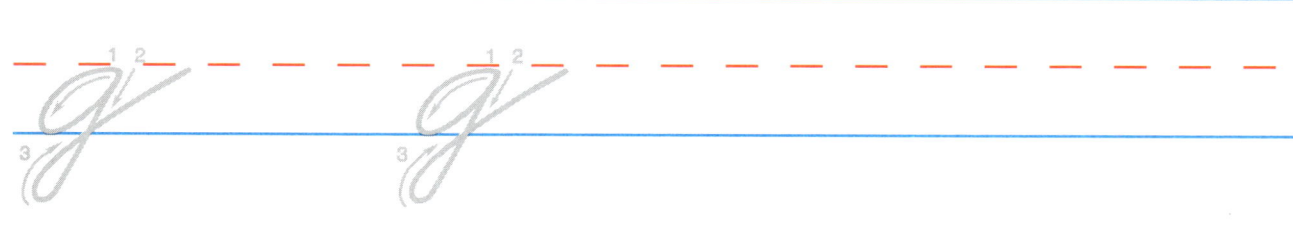

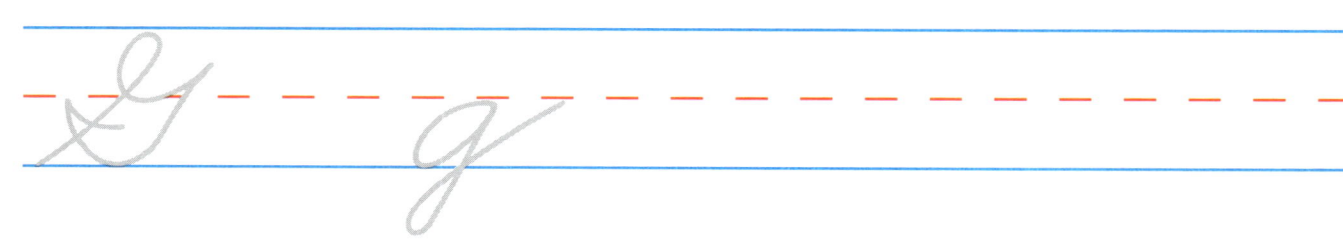

General

Organa

great

Smart Skill: H/h

Han Solo helps the rebels on Hoth.

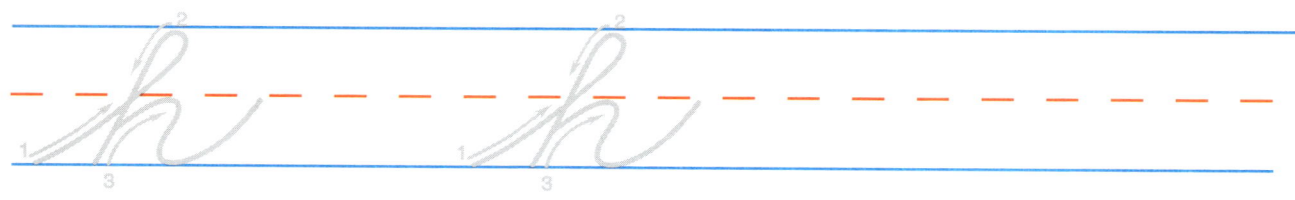

Han Solo

helps

Hoth

Smart Skill: I/i

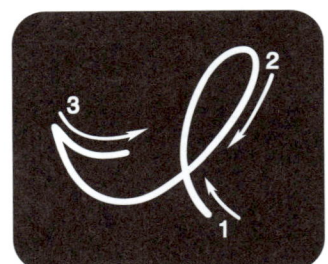

Imperial troops fight the Rebel Alliance.

Imperial troops fight the Rebel Alliance.

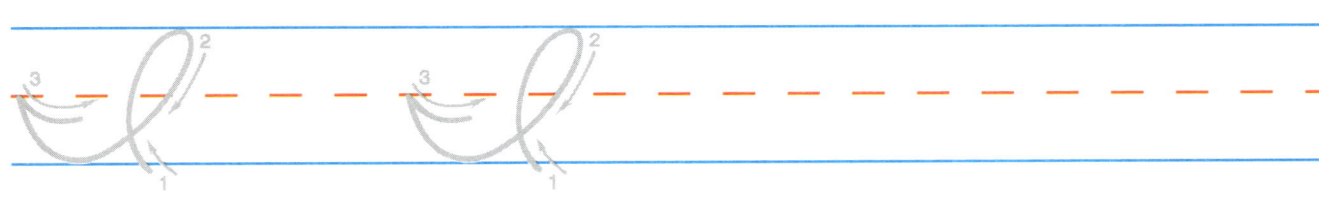

Imperial

fight

Alliance

Smart Skill: J/j

Jannah and her team join Finn.

Jannah and her team join Finn.

Smart Skill: K/k

Kylo Ren leads the First Order.

Kylo Ren leads the First Order.

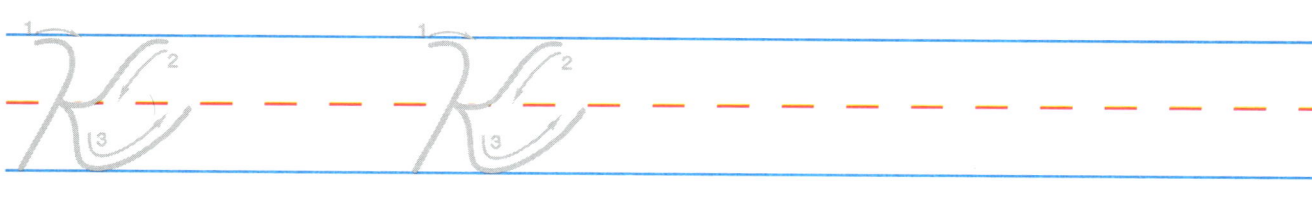

Smart Skill: L/l

Luke Skywalker works on his lightsaber skills.

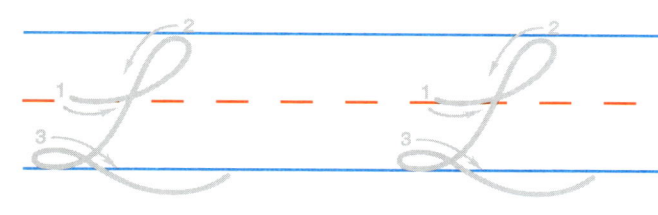

Luke

Skywalker

lightsaber

Smart Skill: M/m

Maz Kanata is a master storyteller.

Maz Kanata

master

Smart Skill: N/n

Naboo's Queen Amidala is young and brave.

Naboo's Queen Amidala is young and brave.

Naboo

Queen

young

Smart Skill: O/o

Obi-Wan Kenobi is one with the Force.

Obi-Wan Kenobi is one with the Force.

Obi-Wan

Kenobi

Force

Smart Skill: P/p

Poe Dameron prepares to pilot his ship.

Poe Dameron prepares to pilot his ship.

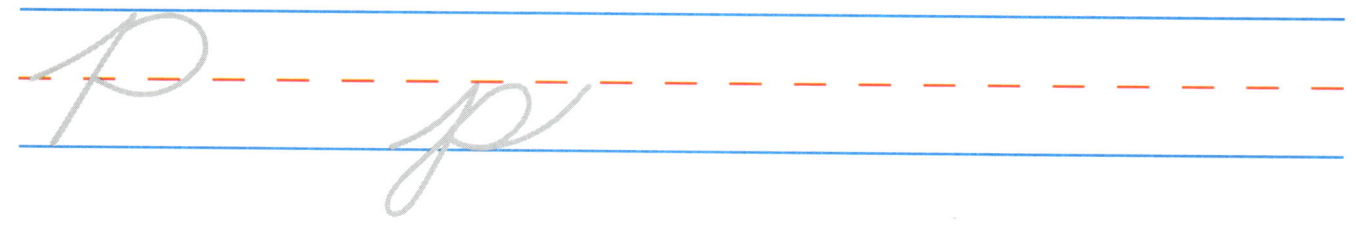

Poe

prepares

pilot

Smart Skill: Q/q

Qui-Gon Jinn is quite skilled.

Qui-Gon Jinn is quite skilled.

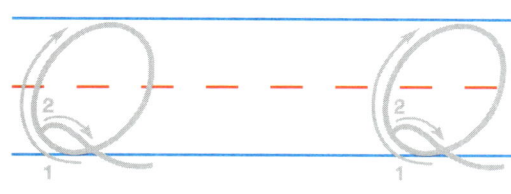

Qui-Gon

quite

Smart Skill: R/r

Rey is ready to fight Kylo Ren.

Rey is ready to fight Kylo Ren.

Rey

ready

Kylo Ren

Smart Skill: S/s

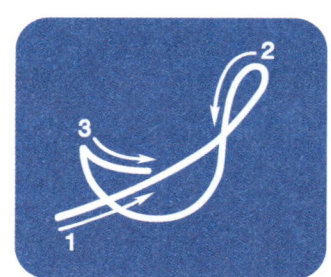

Darth Sidious is a Sith.

Darth Sidious is a Sith.

Sidious

is

Sith

Smart Skill: T/t

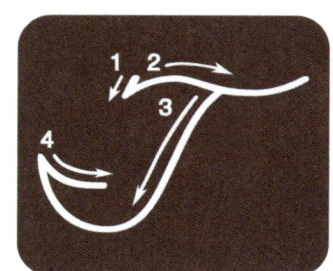

Rose Tico is a Resistance flight technician.

Rose Tico is a Resistance flight technician.

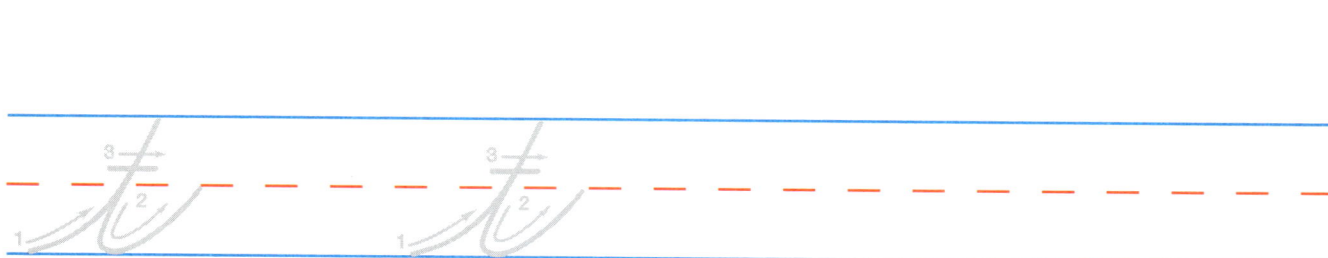

Rose Tico

flight

technician

Smart Skill: U/u

Up flies the Millennium Falcon!

Up flies the Millennium Falcon!

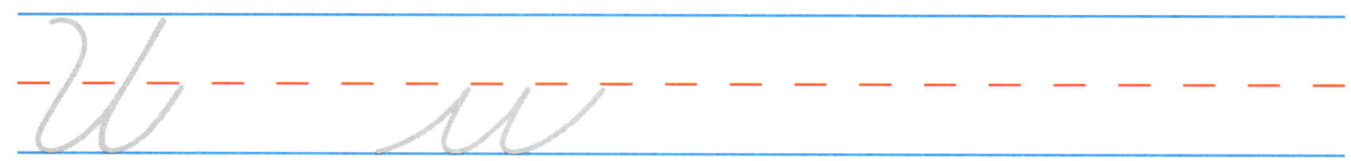

Up

millennium

Smart Skill: V/v

Darth Vader battles his former master, Obi-Wan Kenobi.

Darth Vader battles his former master, Obi-Wan Kenobi.

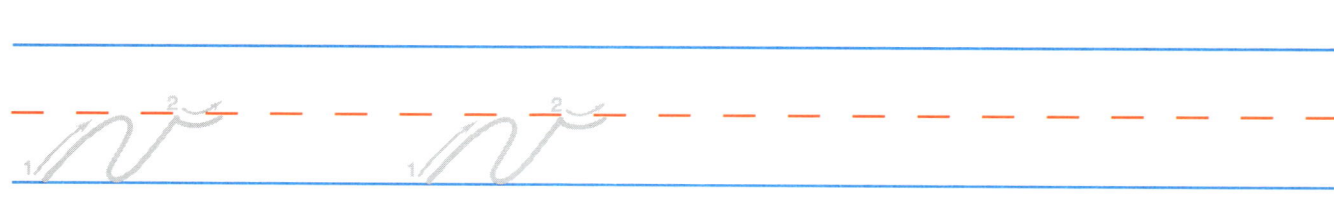

Smart Skill: W/w

Wampas don't live where it is warm.

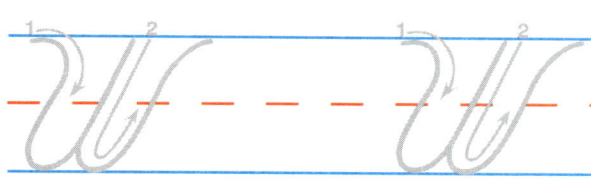

Wampas

where

warm

Smart Skill: X/x

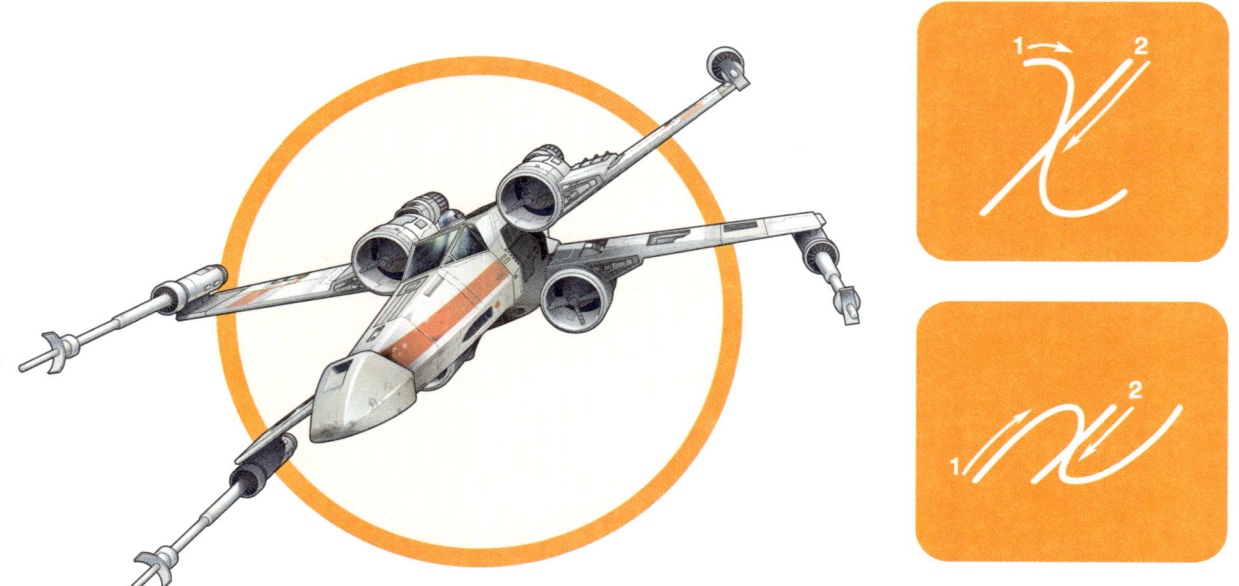

The X-Wing flies at maximum speed.

The X-Wing flies at maximum speed.

X-wing

maximum

Smart Skill: Y/y

Very wise, Yoda is.

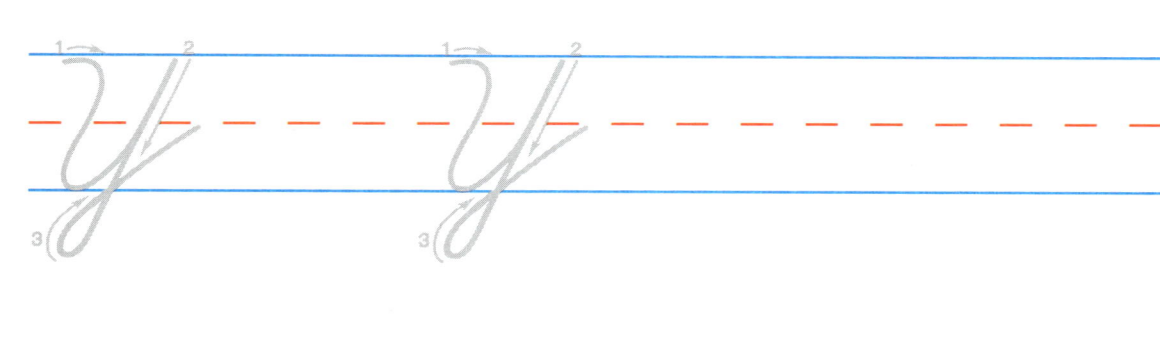

Very

Yoda

Smart Skill: Z/z

Zorii Bliss can zap enemies.

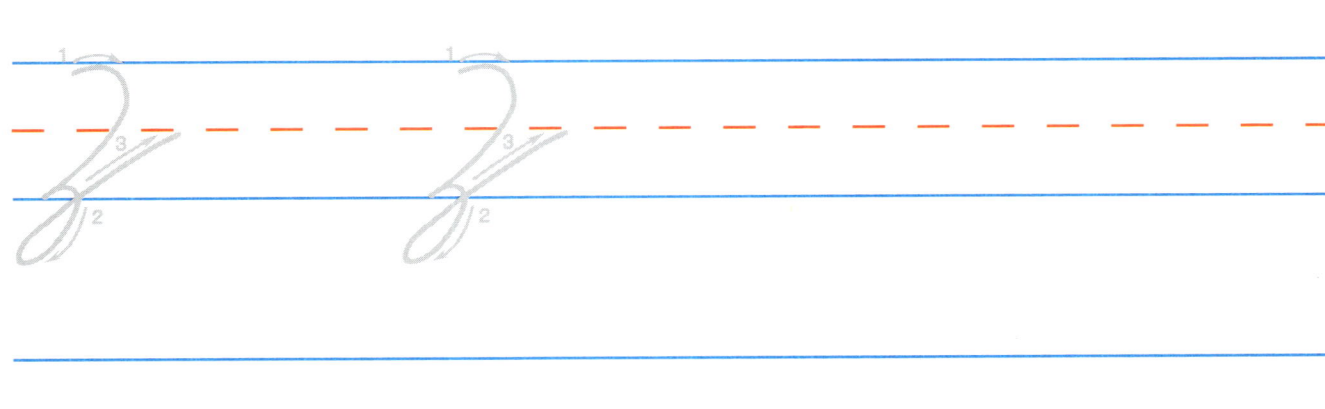

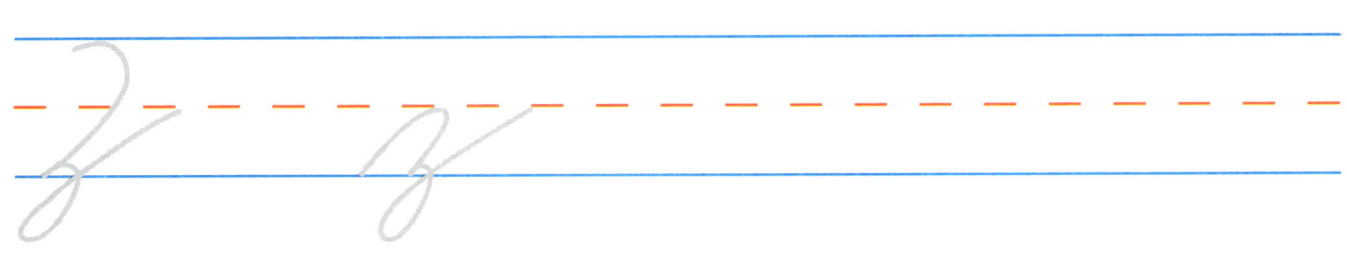

Smart Skill: Missing Letter Practice

Write the missing uppercase or lowercase letter.

Write the missing uppercase or lowercase letter.

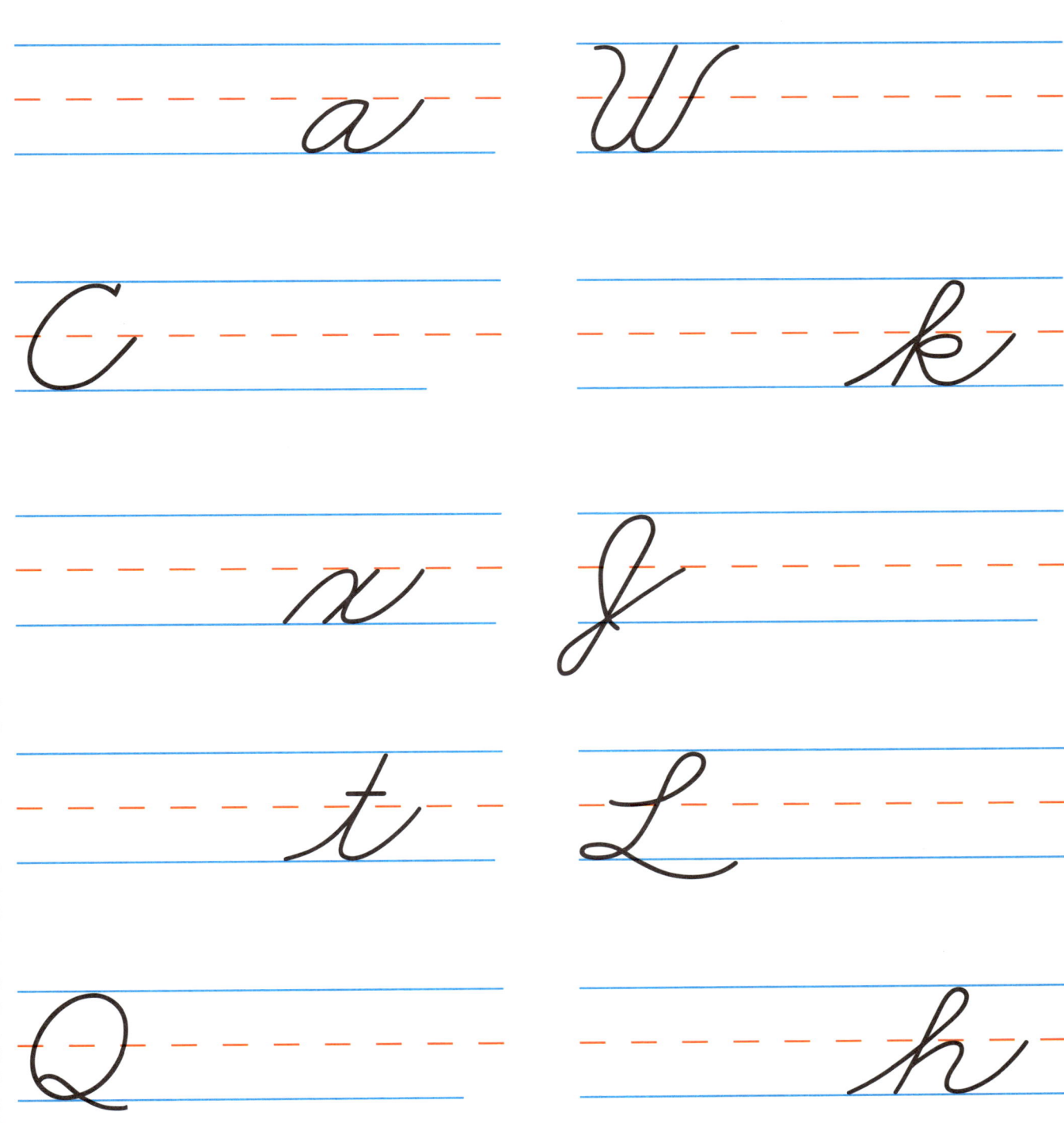

Smart Skill: Word and Sentence Practice

Write a story in cursive that talks about at least one of the characters pictured above.

Write a story in cursive that talks about at least one of the characters pictured above.

Smart Skill: Word and Sentence Practice

Write a story in cursive that talks about at least one of the characters pictured above.

Write a story in cursive that talks about at least one of the characters pictured above.

Congratulations

to

_____

for completing this workbook!

Keep up the good work!